GONE BEFORE MORNING

The Unanswered Case of Asha Degree

Linda Davidson

For Asha— and for every family still waiting for answers.

"Some names become stories. Some stories become prayers."

CONTENTS

Title Page
Dedication
Epigraph
Follow the Author
Preface
The Gone Before Series
Frontispiece Notice
Disclaimer
Introduction
Prologue
Chapter 1 Asha Before the Disappearance   1
Chapter 2 Valentine's Day Weekend   4
Chapter 3 The Walk Along Highway 18   8
Chapter 4 The Missing Child Alarm   11
Chapter 5 The Search Effort   15
Chapter 6 The Shed Discovery   18
Chapter 7 The Backpack Buried   21
Chapter 8 Family Under the Microscope   24
Chapter 9 Theories That Refuse to Die   27
Chapter 10 Persons of Interest and Leads   31
Chapter 11 Media, Memory, and Public Obsession   35

Chapter 12 Law Enforcement Then and Now	38
Chapter 13 What We Know for Certain	41
Chapter 14 The Questions That Haunt	45
Epilogue	49
A Personal Request	53
The Gone Before Series	55
Appendix A — Case Timeline at a Glance	57
Appendix B — Key Locations and Why They Matter	59
Appendix C — Myths vs. Facts	61
Appendix D — How Cold Cases Get Reopened and Solved	63
Appendix E — Facts-Only Narrative Timeline (Report Style)	65
Appendix F — Glossary of Recurring Terms	67
Acknowledgments	71
Disclaimer	73
Author's Note	75
Reader Discretion Statement	77
Notes on Terminology and Approach	79
About the Author	81
Also By Linda Davidson	83
A Final Word to the Reader	85
Follow the Author	87
End Note	89
Appeal for Information	91
How to Report Information	93
A Final Reminder	95
References	97
Further Reading and Viewing	99
Further viewing and listening	101

FOLLOW THE AUTHOR

To explore all of Linda Davidson's books and new releases, visit her Amazon Author Page on Kindle: Linda Davidson.

PREFACE

This book exists because some mysteries do not fade with time—they deepen. They settle into the walls of a community, into the routines of the families who keep living, and into the public imagination where questions repeat themselves without ever finding a place to land.

On February 14, 2000, nine-year-old Asha Degree left her home in Shelby, North Carolina, during a storm and vanished. The details that followed formed a case defined by contradictions so sharp they still feel unreal: a child described as cautious walking alone into rain and darkness; credible sightings that arrived without a rescue; physical evidence that surfaced later, not as a solution but as a new layer of unanswered. The longer the case remained open, the more it gathered what cold cases always gather—rumor, certainty without proof, theories that multiply faster than verifiable facts.

This book is not written to add to that noise.

The goal here is not to force closure where none exists. It is to preserve what can be verified, to separate fact from speculation, and to hold the story with the seriousness it deserves. When a child disappears without a confirmed crime scene, without a confirmed trajectory, without an identified offender, the temptation is to fill the silence with something—anything—that feels like explanation. But explanation is not the same as truth. And when truth is missing, responsibility matters even more.

True crime, handled responsibly, is not entertainment. It is memory. It is documentation. Sometimes it is a quiet form of advocacy—insisting that a missing child's name is still worth saying, that unanswered cases still deserve care, that the lives at the center of them were never "content." They were people. They had voices, habits, fears, favorite things, ordinary days that should have continued.

Asha was not a mystery first. She was a child. She belonged to a family. She had a place in a home, in a community, in a world that expected her to grow up.

Because of that, this book is written with restraint. Certain details are included only where they help clarify the record. Certain rumors are addressed only to prevent them from hardening into misinformation. When sources conflict, the conflict matters—and it is treated as part of the story, not an inconvenience to be smoothed over. Where there are gaps, the gaps are acknowledged honestly. The absence itself is evidence of how difficult this case is, and how careful we must be with what we think we know.

This is also a book about how missing-child cases live in time. How early hours matter. How leads cool. How witness memories shift. How evidence can reappear years later and still refuse to explain itself. And how families endure a kind of waiting that has no calendar.

If you are reading this as someone new to the case, I ask one thing before you go further: hold Asha in your mind as a real person. Not a symbol. Not a story twist. Not a puzzle designed for our satisfaction. A child.

And if you are reading this because you have carried her story for years—returning to it, hoping for clarity—may these pages offer something steady: a careful record, a respectful lens, and a refusal to let her become background.

This book is written in that spirit.

THE GONE BEFORE SERIES

*True Crime Disappearances at
the Edge of Ordinary Time*

Gone Before the Shift Ended: The Unanswered Disappearance of Patti Adkins

A factory worker vanishes after her night shift, leaving behind secrets, suspicion, and a case still clouded in silence.

Gone Before Morning: The Unanswered Case of Asha Degree

A nine-year-old girl walks into the dark before dawn — and is never seen again.

Gone Before Sunrise: The Disappearance of Holly Bobo

A young nursing student is led into the woods at daybreak, sparking one of Tennessee's most haunting investigations.

FRONTISPIECE NOTICE

Asha Degree was nine years old when she disappeared on February 14, 2000.

This book is written in remembrance of her—and in hope that truth still has a way of surfacing.

Appeal for Information

This case remains open. If you have any information related to the disappearance of Asha Degree, please contact law enforcement. Even small details may matter.

DISCLAIMER

This book concerns the disappearance of a child. Some material may be distressing. Reader discretion is advised.

The author does not claim to know what happened to Asha Degree. Where information is uncertain or disputed, the narrative reflects that uncertainty. This book is not intended to accuse any private individual of wrongdoing.

If you have information related to this case, please contact the appropriate law enforcement agency.

INTRODUCTION

The hardest part of an unresolved disappearance is that it refuses to become past tense.

There is no clean ending—only an open space where answers should be. In the Degree family's life, that space began in the early hours of Valentine's Day 2000. In the public's imagination, it began with one haunting image: a child walking alone on a rural highway before dawn, rain falling, headlights catching her shape, and then—sudden movement as she ran into the woods.

Everything after that is fragments.

A backpack wrapped and buried.

A shed where small items appeared.

A timeline that holds steady even as meaning slips away.

This book follows the case as faithfully as possible, beginning where the mystery begins—not in theory, but in the lived reality of a family waking to a missing child and a community searching a storm-soaked landscape.

Because sometimes the only responsible way to tell a story like this is to start with what we can say with certainty:

Asha Degree was here.

And then she wasn't.

PROLOGUE

— *The Girl Who Walked Into the Dark*

In the early hours of February 14, 2000, the roads of rural North Carolina were nearly empty.

The storm had already announced itself hours earlier—cold rain tapping insistently against windows, wind threading through bare trees, power lines humming under strain. Inside modest homes along Highway 18, families slept, unaware that the night was quietly preparing to leave behind a question that would never loosen its grip.

Sometime after 2:30 a.m., a nine-year-old girl stepped out of her house and into the dark.

Her name was .

She did not leave in haste. There was no broken window, no forced door, no sign of panic. She carried a small backpack—packed carefully, deliberately—with clothes and personal items she had chosen herself. She wore a long-sleeved shirt and white sneakers, clothing that offered little protection against the rain or the February cold. The house behind her remained quiet. Inside, her family slept.

Outside, the night swallowed her whole.

Highway 18 stretched ahead like a dark ribbon, slick with rain and reflecting the faint glow of distant headlights. It was not a place for children. Tractor-trailers occasionally thundered through, their engines breaking the silence before disappearing again into the black. The wind pressed low against the fields. Visibility was poor. Even adults would have hesitated to walk there alone.

But Asha did not hesitate.

At some point along the highway, a motorist noticed her. Then another. Drivers later told investigators they were unsettled by the sight—a small figure walking with purpose in the rain, far too young to be out alone at that hour. One driver turned his vehicle around, perhaps intending to help, perhaps simply trying to make sense of what he was seeing.

When the headlights swung back toward her, Asha did not wave. She did not approach.

She ran.

She fled the road and disappeared into the woods.

That moment—brief, silent, and witnessed by strangers who did not yet understand its significance—would become one of the most chilling and confounding details of the case. A child alone. Afraid of help. Choosing darkness over a passing car.

By morning, she was gone.

At dawn, her parents woke expecting a normal Valentine's Day. School was in session. Life was supposed to resume its ordinary rhythm. But when they checked Asha's bed, it was empty. Her jacket was missing. So was her backpack.

Panic set in with a speed that words cannot fully capture.

Calls were made. Neighbors searched. Law enforcement arrived. The house filled with noise, confusion, and rising dread. Within hours, the search expanded beyond the Degree family's yard, beyond their street, beyond anything that could still be contained by hope alone.

Dogs were brought in. Helicopters circled. Volunteers lined the roadside, scanning ditches and tree lines. The rain that had accompanied Asha's departure now worked against those trying to find her, washing away footprints, erasing fragile clues before they could be read.

No body was found.

No clear crime scene revealed itself.

What investigators uncovered instead were fragments—unsettling, incomplete, and deeply contradictory. A child who was afraid of the dark had walked into it. A girl who loved her family had left without waking them. A disappearance that looked nothing like a typical runaway case yet refused to fit neatly into any other category.

As hours turned to days, and days into weeks, the story of Asha Degree spread far beyond her small hometown. Her face appeared on flyers, on television screens, on the front pages of newspapers. She became a symbol of a mystery that resisted explanation, a case that seemed to ask more questions every time someone tried to answer one.

Why did she leave?

Where was she going?

And what happened after she ran from the road and into the trees?

More than two decades later, those questions remain unanswered.

What is known is this: in the span of a single rainy night, a child vanished without a trace that could lead her home. There were witnesses, but no rescue. Evidence, but no resolution. Sightings, but no certainty.

And somewhere between the quiet of her bedroom and the darkness beyond Highway 18, Asha Degree's story slipped into a space where time no longer moves forward—only outward, touching everyone who hears it, and leaving behind a silence that still feels unfinished.

This is not the story of a girl who disappeared.

It is the story of a night that never ended.

CHAPTER 1 ASHA BEFORE THE DISAPPEARANCE

Before she became a name spoken in whispers and headlines, was simply a little girl growing up in a quiet corner of North Carolina.

She lived in Shelby, a small city where neighborhoods blurred into one another and people tended to know who belonged where. Her home sat along Oakcrest Drive, a modest house filled with the ordinary sounds of family life—television murmuring in the background, homework spread across tables, laughter breaking out over small jokes. It was not a house marked by chaos or instability. It was, by all outward measures, safe.

Asha was the youngest child in the Degree family. She shared a bedroom with her older brother, Harold, a detail that would later take on haunting significance. The siblings were close, bonded by routines and rituals that made nighttime less intimidating. They went to bed together, often talking quietly before sleep. Harold later told investigators that Asha was afraid of the dark—so afraid, in fact, that she preferred not to sleep alone. This was not unusual for a child her age, but it stood in stark contrast to what would later unfold.

Those who knew Asha described her as shy but sweet, cautious yet capable. She was polite, respectful, and deeply attached to her family. She followed rules. She listened to adults. Teachers remembered her as a good student—quiet in class, eager to please, not the type to seek attention or rebel. She was not impulsive. She was not defiant. She was not known for secrecy.

If there was one thing that defined Asha, it was reliability.

She attended Fallston Elementary School, where her days followed a predictable rhythm. School, homework, dinner, church activities. Sundays were often spent at services, where faith and community blended into a steady presence in her life. The Degree family was involved and attentive, the kind of parents who knew where their children were and who they were with.

There were no reports of abuse. No history of neglect. No signs of turmoil severe enough to explain a child choosing to leave home in the middle of the night.

Asha loved basketball, even though she wasn't particularly confident on the court. She had recently played in a game where she fouled out, a moment that embarrassed her deeply. Some later wondered if that disappointment weighed on her more than anyone realized. But children face setbacks all the time. They feel embarrassed, frustrated, even ashamed—and then they move on. Nothing in Asha's behavior afterward suggested she was spiraling or planning an escape.

At home, she was affectionate. She followed instructions. She did not argue. She did not test boundaries.

Most importantly, she did not talk about wanting to leave.

In the days leading up to her disappearance, there were no alarming changes. No sudden withdrawal. No secretive behavior.

No goodbye notes hidden away in drawers. Her schoolwork was normal. Her interactions with family were normal. The rhythm of her life remained intact.

That normalcy would become one of the most troubling aspects of the case.

Runaway children often leave clues behind—anger, fear, desperation, a buildup of tension. Asha left nothing of the sort. If she was planning something, she kept it entirely to herself. And for a nine-year-old, that level of secrecy is rare.

She was also not adventurous in the way people often imagine runaway children to be. She did not roam the neighborhood alone. She did not sneak out to meet friends. She was cautious, particularly at night. Storms frightened her. Darkness unsettled her.

Yet something—or someone—managed to override every instinct she had.

When investigators later examined the details of Asha's life, they found no obvious cracks. No motive large enough to explain why a child like her would pack a bag, wait until the house was asleep, and walk into a cold, stormy night.

The absence of explanation became its own kind of presence.

It forced investigators, journalists, and the public to confront a deeply uncomfortable truth: sometimes, the most disturbing mysteries are born not from chaos, but from calm. From families doing their best. From children who seem happy, loved, and secure.

Asha Degree did not fit the profile of a child who disappears voluntarily.

Which raises the question that would haunt everyone who came to know her story:

If she didn't leave because she wanted to—

what made her go?

CHAPTER 2
VALENTINE'S DAY WEEKEND

The weekend leading into Valentine's Day in 2000 unfolded without warning of what was to come.

Sunday, February 13, was ordinary in the way families rarely think to remember. attended church with her family, dressed neatly, behaving as she always did. There were no tearful moments, no resistance to going, no signs of distress that stood out in hindsight. To those around her, she appeared calm, present, and very much herself.

Later that afternoon, the Degrees returned home and settled into the familiar cadence of a school night. Homework was completed. Dinner was eaten. The television flickered in the background as the evening wound down. Valentine's Day fell on a Monday that year, which meant no late-night excitement, no parties, no reason to stay up beyond routine.

But the night would not remain routine for long.

At some point that evening, a storm began to move through the area. Rain fell steadily, accompanied by gusts of wind strong enough to rattle windows and sway trees. Around 9:00 p.m., the power went out. The house was suddenly quiet, illuminated only by candles and flashlights. For children—especially those afraid of the dark—this kind of disruption could be unsettling.

Still, nothing appeared out of place.

Asha and her brother Harold eventually went to bed in their shared room. Harold later recalled that they talked for a while before falling asleep, as they often did. There was no argument. No unusual conversation. No sense that Asha was restless or anxious. When sleep finally came, it did so quietly.

Sometime after midnight, the power returned. The lights came back on. The television resumed its low hum. In many homes, this moment passed unnoticed. In the Degree household, it marked one of the last clearly remembered moments before everything fractured.

Investigators later pieced together a narrow window of time in which Asha likely left the house—sometime between 2:30 and 3:30 a.m.

She did not wake her brother.

She did not alert her parents.

She did not leave a note.

Instead, she gathered her belongings with care. Clothing. Personal items. Things that suggested planning rather than impulse. The backpack she carried was not random—it was purposeful. Whatever she believed she was doing, she thought she would need supplies.

The front door closed behind her without sound.

Outside, the storm was still active. Rain slicked the pavement. The temperature hovered uncomfortably low for a child dressed lightly. The neighborhood was silent, most residents unaware that a nine-year-old was passing through the darkness alone.

What compelled her to leave at that hour remains one of the case's most disturbing unknowns.

Children who run away typically leave during daylight hours or in moments of heightened emotion—after an argument, a punishment, a confrontation. Asha left while her family slept, choosing a time when discovery would be delayed and help would be unlikely.

Equally unsettling was where she did not go.

She did not head toward a friend's house. She did not walk to a familiar location. Instead, she turned onto Highway 18, a stretch of road that offered no comfort, no shelter, and no clear destination for a child on foot.

By the time her parents awoke later that morning, the window to stop her had long closed.

They noticed her bed was empty. Her coat was missing. Panic took hold almost instantly. A child does not simply vanish from a locked house in the middle of the night—not without reason, and not without consequence.

As daylight spread across Shelby, fear replaced confusion. Family members searched the house again and again, hoping she had simply gone to the bathroom or climbed into another bed. When that hope collapsed, the calls began—to relatives, to neighbors, to the police.

Within hours, Valentine's Day ceased to be a holiday.

It became the marker of a before and an after.

For investigators, the events of that night would become the foundation of every theory, every lead, every dead end. The timeline was narrow but devastatingly opaque. Too much happened while no one was watching. Too many crucial moments passed in silence.

A child had left her home willingly—or under influence—into a storm, into darkness, into a future that remains unknown.

And whatever happened next began on a night that should have been forgettable, but never would be.

CHAPTER 3 THE WALK ALONG HIGHWAY 18

Highway 18 is not a road built for wandering.

It cuts through Cleveland County with long, unbroken stretches bordered by fields, trees, and scattered homes set far back from the pavement. At night—especially in bad weather—it becomes a narrow corridor of darkness, illuminated only by the occasional sweep of headlights. There are no sidewalks. No streetlamps. No safe places for a child to pause and gather courage.

Yet sometime in the early hours of February 14, 2000, walked along it alone.

Investigators would later determine that she likely left her house on Oakcrest Drive and made her way toward the highway on foot. The distance was not insignificant for a nine-year-old, particularly in the rain. Each step carried her farther from the safety of home and deeper into isolation.

At approximately 3:45 a.m., the first motorist noticed her.

The driver was traveling southbound when headlights caught

something unexpected on the shoulder of the road—a small figure walking against traffic. At first, the driver thought it might be a woman, perhaps a teenager. As the vehicle drew closer, the realization set in: this was a child. Alone. In the rain.

Unnerved, the driver continued on, unsure of what he had just seen.

A short time later, another motorist encountered the same sight. This time, the reaction was stronger. The driver turned the vehicle around, attempting to get a better look. There was concern—confusion mixed with a sense that something was deeply wrong.

When the headlights swept back toward the girl, she reacted instantly.

She ran.

Not toward the road. Not toward help. She bolted away from the light, leaving the shoulder and plunging into the dark woods that bordered the highway. The trees swallowed her quickly, their bare branches and undergrowth offering concealment but no comfort.

The driver did not pursue her on foot. In the moment, fear and uncertainty won out. The incident was later reported to authorities, but by then the trail was already cooling.

That brief encounter—lasting only seconds—would become one of the most haunting elements of the case.

Children who are lost or in distress typically respond to adults with relief. They wave. They cry. They ask for help. Asha did the opposite. Her instinct was flight. Whatever was driving her forward made the approaching car more frightening than the storm, the cold, or the darkness.

Why?

Some have suggested she was taught not to trust strangers, a lesson many children are carefully given. Others believe she may have been frightened by something else entirely—something that made stopping feel dangerous. There is also the unsettling possibility that she believed she was where she was supposed to be, and that interference would ruin a plan she felt compelled to complete.

The road itself offered no clues. Rain continued to fall, erasing footprints almost as quickly as they formed. Any trace of her presence—mud, impressions, disturbed gravel—vanished beneath the weather.

What happened after she ran into the woods is unknown.

Search teams would later scour the area where she was last seen, but they found nothing definitive. No clothing. No blood. No sign of struggle. It was as though she had stepped off the road and out of existence.

The eyewitness accounts were credible. Multiple drivers reported seeing a child matching Asha's description at roughly the same location and time. Their statements aligned. The timeline held.

And yet, credibility did not bring clarity.

Instead, it deepened the mystery.

Asha had made it miles from her home on foot, in the middle of the night, during a storm. She had done so without alerting anyone, without being intercepted, and without leaving behind evidence that could explain what happened next.

The highway marked the last confirmed sighting of her alive.

Beyond that point, there is only speculation.

Whatever pulled her from her bed and onto that road did not release its hold when fear should have stopped her. Even when a car slowed, even when help was within reach, she chose the unknown over safety.

And somewhere beyond the edge of Highway 18, the trail ended—not with answers, but with silence.

CHAPTER 4 THE MISSING CHILD ALARM

Morning arrived quietly on Oakcrest Drive, unaware of the urgency it would soon carry.

It was Monday, February 14, 2000—Valentine's Day. A school day. A day meant to follow routine. Inside the Degree home, the first moments after waking were unremarkable, until they weren't.

When Asha's parents went to check on the children, her bed was empty.

At first, confusion softened the fear. Perhaps she had gone to the bathroom. Perhaps she had climbed into another room. They called her name. They searched the house. Each unanswered call sharpened the panic. Asha's jacket was missing. Her backpack was gone.

This was not forgetfulness. This was absence.

Within minutes, dread replaced denial. A child did not simply walk out of the house unnoticed—especially not Asha. She was afraid of the dark. Afraid of storms. Afraid of being alone at night.

Every instinct her parents had told them something was terribly wrong.

The first calls went out quickly—to relatives, to neighbors, to anyone who might have seen her. No one had. The neighborhood was still shaking off sleep, doors opening to confusion as word spread. Soon after, law enforcement was contacted.

By the time officers arrived, the Degree home had transformed from a private space into the center of an emergency. Questions filled the air. When was she last seen? What was she wearing? Did she say anything unusual? Had there been arguments? Punishments? Threats to run away?

The answers were all the same.

No.

No.

Nothing.

Investigators moved swiftly, aware of the unforgiving nature of time in missing child cases. The longer a child is gone, the colder the trail becomes. They searched the house carefully, looking for signs of forced entry, struggle, or planning. They found none.

The doors were locked. Windows intact.

There was no note.

As the hours passed, the reality set in: had left on her own—or under circumstances that left no immediate trace.

Search efforts expanded rapidly. Officers canvassed the neighborhood, knocking on doors, asking if anyone had heard or seen anything during the night. Most had not. The storm had kept people indoors. The darkness had concealed movement.

Then, the first break came—not from a searcher on foot, but from the road.

A motorist contacted authorities to report something unsettling: earlier that morning, before dawn, they had seen a child walking along Highway 18. Another driver soon corroborated the sighting, adding the detail that the child had run into the woods when approached.

The reports changed everything.

This was no longer a case of a child who might be hiding nearby. Asha had traveled far enough to be seen by strangers, on a dangerous highway, in the middle of the night. The search radius widened instantly.

K-9 units were deployed. Helicopters took to the air. Volunteers poured in—hundreds of them—walking fields, checking ditches, calling her name into the trees. Church members, neighbors, and strangers joined forces, bound together by urgency and disbelief.

But the storm had done its damage.

Rain had washed away footprints. Wind had scattered scent. The very conditions that made Asha's walk so perilous now worked against those trying to find her. Dogs struggled. Searchers found nothing definitive—no clothing, no blood, no clear path into the woods.

As the day wore on, optimism thinned.

Investigators faced a case that refused to settle into any known pattern. There was no ransom demand. No witnesses to an abduction. No history of family conflict. No indication that Asha had planned to disappear forever.

And yet, she was gone.

By nightfall, the missing child alert had spread far beyond Shelby. Her name reached television screens, radio broadcasts, and neighboring states. Her face—young, smiling, unaware of the role it would play—began to circulate in the public eye.

For her family, time stopped moving forward. Every sound outside carried hope and dread in equal measure. Every phone call felt like it could change everything.

But none did.

Valentine's Day ended not with flowers or cards, but with unanswered questions and a growing realization: whatever had taken Asha from her home had already placed her beyond reach.

And the clock, merciless and silent, kept ticking.

CHAPTER 5 THE SEARCH EFFORT

By the second day, Shelby no longer felt like a small town.

It felt like a command center.

Roads filled with law enforcement vehicles from multiple agencies. Churches opened their doors to volunteers. Folding tables appeared, covered with maps, radios, and sign-in sheets. The search for had grown into a massive operation, fueled by urgency and a collective refusal to believe a child could simply vanish.

Search crews focused first on the area surrounding Highway 18, where the last confirmed sightings had occurred. Teams walked shoulder to shoulder through fields and wooded patches, eyes trained on the ground for anything out of place. Ditches were checked. Culverts examined. Ponds scanned for disturbance. Every scrap of fabric, every footprint-shaped indentation in the mud drew attention—then disappointment.

K-9 units returned again and again, trying to pick up a usable scent. But the storm had erased most of what could have guided them. Rain had soaked the ground, blending scents together, confusing even the most experienced dogs. Trails faded abruptly, ending without explanation.

Helicopters hovered overhead, their low thrum echoing across farmland. From above, officers searched for signs invisible at ground level—movement, broken branches, anything that suggested a child might be hiding or injured. They found nothing.

Volunteers came in waves. Some had children Asha's age. Others simply couldn't stay home knowing a child was missing. They wore bright vests, carried whistles, and called her name until their voices grew hoarse.

"Asha!"

"Asha, it's okay!"

"Come out—we're here!"

The words drifted through the woods, unanswered.

As the days stretched on, searchers expanded outward, following every plausible route a child could have taken. They walked miles of roadside. They checked abandoned buildings. They knocked on doors far from the Degree home, asking residents if they had noticed anything unusual in the early hours of Valentine's Day.

Most had not.

The absence of physical evidence became its own kind of message—one investigators struggled to interpret. Children who wander off are usually found nearby, tired, cold, hiding, or injured. Children who are abducted often leave signs of struggle or witnesses to a sudden event.

Asha's case offered neither.

No torn clothing.

No blood.

No confirmed destination.

The community clung to hope in small ways. A reported sighting here. A possible lead there. Each one briefly reignited momentum, only to collapse under scrutiny. One tip suggested she had been picked up by a passing vehicle. Another claimed she had been seen at a local store. None could be verified.

Behind the scenes, investigators faced growing pressure. Every hour that passed without progress made recovery less likely. Media attention intensified. Reporters gathered near the Degree home, broadcasting updates that felt painfully thin.

For Asha's family, the search was both comfort and torment.

Seeing strangers comb the land for their child offered proof that she had not been forgotten. But each failed sweep, each returned volunteer, carried the same silent question: if she were here, wouldn't someone have found her by now?

As night fell again, search efforts slowed but did not stop. Officers continued to patrol. Phones stayed on. The hope that Asha might still be alive—cold, frightened, but waiting—refused to die.

Yet beneath that hope, a darker possibility began to take shape.

The longer the search went on without results, the harder it became to believe she was simply lost.

And in the spaces where evidence should have been, investigators were left to confront a reality they did not want to name: whatever had happened to Asha may not have happened in the open.

It may have happened where no one was looking.

CHAPTER 6 THE SHED DISCOVERY

The first tangible trace of did not come from the road, the woods, or the massive search efforts that had consumed Cleveland County.

It came from a place no one initially thought to look.

Several days after Asha vanished, a property owner came forward with information that would redirect the investigation in a troubling new direction. On his land, just off Highway 18, stood a small, weathered storage shed—little more than a makeshift outbuilding, open to the elements and rarely used. It sat near the area where witnesses had last seen Asha run into the woods.

Inside the shed, searchers found items that did not belong there.

Among them were candy wrappers, a pencil, and other small objects consistent with a child's belongings. They were unremarkable on their own—easily overlooked, easily dismissed —but in the context of the case, they were chilling. These were not items scattered by animals or left by workers. They suggested presence. Brief shelter. A pause.

For the first time since Asha disappeared, investigators had something that felt solid.

The shed became a focal point. Forensic teams examined it carefully, documenting every surface, every corner, every trace of disturbance. The ground around it was checked for footprints or drag marks. The surrounding area was searched again, more intensely than before.

But once again, the evidence refused to cooperate.

No fingerprints conclusively tied to Asha were recovered. No DNA provided answers. There were no signs of a struggle, no blood, no indication that anyone else had been there with her. The items found suggested she may have sought refuge—possibly from the storm, possibly from fear—but they did not explain what happened next.

One detail in particular unsettled investigators.

Among the items was a photograph of an unidentified girl. It was not Asha. The image appeared intentionally placed, not discarded accidentally. Its presence raised immediate questions: Where did it come from? Why was it there? Was it meant to be comforting—or was it a message?

Despite extensive efforts, the girl in the photograph was never definitively identified. The image became one of the most enigmatic pieces of the case, sparking speculation that ranged from innocent coincidence to deliberate manipulation.

Did Asha find the photo?

Did someone leave it there for her?

Or was it connected to something far more sinister?

The shed discovery reshaped the narrative.

Up until that point, it was still possible to believe Asha had wandered aimlessly, perhaps becoming lost or injured in the woods. The shed suggested something different: intention.

Decision-making. A child who had stopped, rested, and then moved on—or been moved.

It also raised a deeply troubling possibility.

If Asha had reached the shed safely, if she had survived the walk along the highway and the flight into the woods, then whatever happened to her occurred *after* that moment. After she had already beaten the odds once.

Search teams returned to the area with renewed urgency, expanding outward again. But the trail did not continue beyond the shed. No further items were found. No direction could be established.

The evidence ended there.

For investigators, the shed became both a breakthrough and a dead end. It confirmed Asha's presence in the area beyond doubt—but it offered no clue as to how she left it, or with whom.

As days turned into weeks, the shed faded from headlines but not from the case file. It remained a quiet, unsettling marker in the timeline—a place where Asha had been, briefly, before vanishing completely.

Whatever happened to her, it did not happen there.

And that realization only deepened the mystery.

CHAPTER 7 THE BACKPACK BURIED

For more than a year after disappeared, the case lived in a painful state of suspension.

Leads came in sporadically. Sightings were reported and dismissed. Theories circulated quietly among investigators and loudly in public spaces. But nothing tangible surfaced—no proof of life, no confirmation of death, no clue strong enough to push the case forward.

Then, in August 2001, eighteen months after Asha vanished, the silence broke.

A construction worker was clearing land in Burke County, more than twenty-five miles north of Shelby, when he noticed something unusual in the dirt. Buried near a roadside construction site was a backpack—sealed inside two black plastic trash bags.

The discovery was immediately reported.

When law enforcement arrived and carefully opened the bags,

the weight of the moment settled in. The backpack was intact. Preserved. Protected from the elements in a way that suggested intention.

It belonged to Asha.

Inside were items that confirmed the identification—school supplies, personal belongings, things she had packed herself on the night she left home. Some items were missing. Others were unfamiliar, including clothing that was not hers.

The location alone stunned investigators.

Asha had last been seen walking along Highway 18 near her home. The backpack was found far from that route, in a different county, along a road she had no known connection to. There was no logical reason for it to be there—unless someone else had put it there.

And that implication changed everything.

The careful burial of the backpack suggested concealment, not accident. This was not something that had been dropped and forgotten. It had been deliberately hidden, wrapped to protect it, placed underground in a location unlikely to be discovered by chance.

For the first time, the possibility of foul play moved from speculation to likelihood.

Yet even this discovery refused to provide answers.

There were no fingerprints that led to an arrest. No DNA that could be conclusively tied to a suspect. The unfamiliar items inside the bag raised questions investigators could not resolve. Were they meant to disguise ownership? Were they placed there to mislead? Or did they belong to someone Asha had encountered?

The backpack told a story—but not enough of one.

For Asha's family, the discovery was devastating in a way that defied language. Hope and grief collided. The bag proved she had survived long enough for it to be moved. But it also suggested she had not returned home. It was proof of absence, wrapped in plastic.

Public attention surged again. Media outlets revisited the case. Old tips were reexamined. New ones poured in. Investigators retraced timelines, reevaluated suspects, and reconsidered theories that had once seemed unlikely.

Still, no clear path emerged.

The backpack became a symbol of the case's cruelty: just enough evidence to confirm that something terrible had happened, but not enough to explain what—or to whom.

Asha had walked into the dark and vanished.

Now, a piece of her had resurfaced—carefully hidden, miles away, carrying silence instead of truth.

And once again, the trail ended.

Not with resolution—but with deeper uncertainty.

CHAPTER 8 FAMILY UNDER THE MICROSCOPE

When a child disappears without witnesses, without a clear suspect, and without immediate evidence of abduction, attention almost always turns inward.

It is an unspoken rule of missing child investigations: before law enforcement looks far away, they look close. And for the Degree family, that meant becoming the focus of intense scrutiny at the most vulnerable moment of their lives.

From the earliest hours of the investigation, detectives interviewed Asha's parents repeatedly. They asked about discipline, arguments, punishments, and family dynamics. They examined routines, bedtime rules, and household structure. Every detail—no matter how mundane—was documented, analyzed, and questioned.

It was necessary.

It was also devastating.

Friends and neighbors initially rallied around the family, offering food, prayers, and support. But as days turned into weeks and Asha did not come home, suspicion began to creep in from outside the inner circle. Whispers surfaced. Comment sections filled. Armchair theories spread, many of them pointing toward the people who loved her most.

This was not unusual. It was the pattern.

Investigators administered polygraph tests. Family members cooperated fully. They answered the same questions again and again, hoping consistency would prove what they already knew—that they had nothing to hide.

And eventually, law enforcement reached a conclusion.

The Degree family was not responsible for Asha's disappearance.

There was no evidence of abuse. No indication of violence. No motive uncovered that could explain why they would harm or hide their own child. Their accounts aligned. Their grief was real. Their cooperation never wavered.

Still, the damage of suspicion lingered.

Living under the weight of public doubt compounded the trauma of loss. Every interview, every media appearance required composure under scrutiny. They were expected to grieve correctly, to speak carefully, to embody the image of victims in a way the public would accept.

Any deviation—too calm, too emotional, too quiet—was analyzed.

The family had not only lost Asha. They had lost privacy, safety, and the right to mourn without being watched.

For investigators, clearing the family did not end the problem—it complicated it. If the disappearance did not begin at home, then it began somewhere between the front door and the highway. And that space, both physical and temporal, was painfully small.

How had a child left without being heard?

Why had no one seen her earlier?

And how had she managed to get so far before anyone realized she was gone?

These questions pushed the investigation outward again, but without a clear direction. Attention shifted to possible external influences—someone who may have known Asha, someone who may have spoken to her before that night, someone who may have gained her trust.

Yet no such person emerged.

No suspicious adults in her life were identified. No evidence surfaced of grooming or secret communication. Teachers, coaches, church leaders—all were questioned. None raised red flags.

The family remained, in the public eye, even after being officially cleared.

For them, time did not heal—it stretched. Every anniversary reopened the wound. Every false lead stirred hope only to crush it again. They continued to speak out, to keep Asha's name alive, even as years passed without answers.

Their endurance became part of the story.

Not as suspects—but as parents and siblings living in the long aftermath of an unanswered question.

And as the investigation moved forward, one truth became unavoidable:

whatever happened to Asha Degree did not begin with malice at home.

It began somewhere else.

CHAPTER 9 THEORIES THAT REFUSE TO DIE

When facts are scarce, theories rush in to fill the silence.

In the case of , speculation became both a tool and a torment—fueling investigation while muddying public understanding. Over the years, certain explanations have resurfaced again and again, refusing to fade no matter how often they are questioned.

Each theory attempts to answer the same impossible question: *why did she leave?*

And each one fractures under scrutiny.

The Runaway Theory

On paper, it is the simplest explanation.

Asha packed a bag. She left voluntarily. She walked away from home.

But nearly every known detail of her personality undermines this idea.

She was nine years old. She was deeply attached to her family. She was afraid of the dark, afraid of storms, afraid of being alone at night. There was no history of defiance, no expressed desire to leave, no secret plans shared with friends.

Runaways typically flee *from* something—abuse, conflict, punishment. Investigators found no evidence of any such trigger. And runaways rarely choose the worst possible conditions to leave: a stormy winter night, hours before school, with no transportation and no clear destination.

The backpack complicates the theory further. Its careful burial suggests someone wanted to hide it—not something a child planning to disappear forever would likely do herself.

The runaway explanation explains movement.

It does not explain motive.

The Grooming or Luring Scenario

This theory has gained traction over time—and for unsettling reasons.

Could someone have gained Asha's trust? Could she have been promised something compelling enough to override fear? A gift, an adventure, a secret, a ride?

Children who are groomed often leave quietly, believing they are meeting someone safe. They follow instructions. They keep secrets.

But investigators found no evidence of such contact.

There were no letters. No phone calls. No internet use. No known adult in her life who raised suspicion. No one reported unusual interactions in the days or weeks before she vanished.

That absence does not eliminate the theory—but it weakens it.

If grooming occurred, it happened without leaving a trace.

Abduction by a Stranger

The buried backpack strongly supports the possibility that Asha encountered someone after leaving home.

A passing driver. Someone familiar with the area. Someone who saw a child alone on the road and seized the opportunity.

But this theory struggles with timing and behavior.

Why would a child abducted by force leave no signs of struggle? Why would no one hear or see anything? And how would a stranger know where to bury the backpack—far from the original search area—in a way that avoided discovery for over a year?

The eyewitness account complicates this further. Asha ran from a car. She did not approach it. That suggests she was not willingly getting into a vehicle at that moment.

Unless the person she feared was not a stranger at all.

Accidental Death and Concealment

Some theories suggest Asha may have suffered an accident after leaving the road—falling, becoming injured, or succumbing to exposure—and that her belongings were later moved to avoid responsibility.

But again, the evidence resists this explanation.

Search teams thoroughly covered the area. Dogs, helicopters, volunteers—nothing was found. And the careful wrapping and burial of the backpack suggests deliberate concealment, not panic or improvisation.

Accidents rarely come with plastic bags and foresight.

Why None of Them Fit

What makes the Asha Degree case endure is not the number of theories—it is the way each one collapses under the weight of the facts.

She was too young to plan an escape.

Too cautious to wander blindly.

Too afraid to seek help from strangers.

Too prepared for the disappearance to be accidental.

Each explanation answers one question while creating five more.

And so the theories persist—not because they are convincing, but because the truth has not replaced them.

They remain suspended in the absence of resolution, circling the same evidence, drawing new lines between old facts, hoping one day something will finally connect.

Until then, the case exists in an uneasy space between possibility and proof—where nothing can be ruled out completely, and nothing can be confirmed.

And at the center of it all is a child whose decision to step into the night still refuses to be explained.

CHAPTER 10 PERSONS OF INTEREST AND LEADS

As the years passed and the case refused to close, investigators were left with little choice but to follow every lead—no matter how thin, delayed, or uncertain.

In the absence of a clear suspect, the investigation into became a long exercise in patience and restraint. Tips arrived from across the country. Some came from people who believed they had seen her. Others came from individuals convinced they knew who was responsible. Most led nowhere.

But each one had to be examined.

Eyewitness Tips and Reported Sightings

In the months and years following Asha's disappearance, law

enforcement received numerous reports of children matching her description. Sightings were claimed in shopping centers, along highways, and in neighboring states. Some callers were earnest, shaken by what they believed they had seen. Others were mistaken, their memories reshaped by media exposure and time.

Each report was investigated.

None were confirmed.

Asha's face had become widely known, and that familiarity created its own problems. Children who resembled her were inadvertently pulled into the orbit of the case, while genuine sightings—if any ever occurred—were impossible to verify without supporting evidence.

Vehicles of Interest

One of the most persistent avenues of inquiry involved vehicles seen in the area around the time Asha disappeared.

Investigators released information about specific vehicle descriptions years later, hoping someone might remember a detail they had once dismissed. Older model cars. Trucks seen parked along roadsides. Vehicles reported by tipsters who only realized their significance after hearing Asha's story.

Time, however, proved unforgiving.

Memories faded. Owners moved or passed away. Vehicles were sold, destroyed, or altered. Even when tips seemed promising, they arrived too late to be actionable.

Local and Regional Leads

Law enforcement also examined known offenders in the region —individuals with histories of violence, abduction, or crimes against children. Some were questioned. Others were ruled out. A few remain quietly noted in files, neither cleared nor charged.

But no single name emerged with enough evidence to withstand scrutiny.

This absence of a clear person of interest frustrated both investigators and the public. In many cases, cold investigations crystallize around one suspect. Asha's case refused to do so.

Instead, it remained fragmented—spread across counties, years, and incomplete information.

Anonymous Tips and Confessions

From time to time, anonymous callers claimed knowledge of what happened to Asha. Some alleged confessions. Others offered vague suggestions or secondhand stories. A few appeared credible enough to warrant deeper examination.

None led to an arrest.

False confessions, exaggerations, and outright hoaxes are an unfortunate reality in high-profile cases. Each one consumed time and resources, drawing investigators away from more promising avenues—yet ignoring them was not an option.

Every claim had to be checked. Every possibility had to be eliminated.

Why the Leads Went Cold

The problem was never a lack of information.

It was the lack of *verifiable* information.

No physical evidence connected a suspect to Asha. No witness placed her with a specific individual after she left the highway. No forensic breakthrough bridged the gap between her disappearance and the buried backpack.

What remained was a case built on fragments—credible but incomplete, suggestive but unprovable.

And so, despite decades of effort, the investigation settled into an uneasy state: open, active, but stalled.

Asha Degree's file is not closed.

It waits—quietly, persistently—for the one lead that will finally hold.

CHAPTER 11 MEDIA, MEMORY, AND PUBLIC OBSESSION

Long after the search teams packed up and the headlines thinned, remained.

Her story did not fade into the background the way many missing-person cases do. Instead, it settled into public memory—quietly at first, then with increasing persistence. Each anniversary brought renewed attention. Each new generation of true crime audiences rediscovered her name and asked the same questions investigators had been asking for years.

Why did she leave?

Where did she go?

How could a child vanish so completely?

Television specials revisited the case. Podcasts dissected timelines. Online forums dedicated thousands of posts to theories, maps, and minute details pulled from decades-old reports. Amateur investigators scrutinized photographs, weather records, and school schedules, hoping to uncover something professionals had missed.

In some ways, this attention kept the case alive.

Public awareness ensured that Asha was not forgotten, that her face remained recognizable, that tips—however rare—continued to come in. Law enforcement acknowledged that media exposure helped maintain pressure and occasionally sparked new leads.

But there was another side to that attention.

Speculation often crossed into certainty. Theories hardened into accusations. Individuals tangentially connected to the case found themselves named, dissected, and condemned without evidence. The Degree family, though officially cleared long ago, continued to face invasive scrutiny from strangers convinced they had uncovered "the truth."

True crime culture blurred lines that were once clearer.

What began as a search for answers sometimes transformed into entertainment—narratives shaped for engagement rather than accuracy. Details were misquoted. Timelines distorted. Rumors repeated until they sounded factual.

And yet, people kept looking.

Asha's case occupies a particular place in the true crime landscape because it defies resolution. There is no known crime scene. No identified suspect. No definitive explanation. The mystery is clean in its cruelty—nothing messy enough to solve, nothing clear enough to close.

That uncertainty invites obsession.

For many, the case becomes personal. Parents imagine their own children walking into the night. Former children imagine what fear—or faith—might have driven them to do the same. Each person projects a different story onto the same empty space.

But behind the headlines and theories, a real family continues to live with the consequences of that obsession.

They do not have the luxury of stepping away from the case when interest wanes. They carry it into every year, every milestone Asha never reached. They watch her story be retold, reshaped, and sometimes mishandled—knowing that remembrance is both a gift and a burden.

The media can preserve memory.

It can also distort it.

And in the case of Asha Degree, the line between awareness and appropriation has never been easy to draw. The public continues to search for meaning in her disappearance, even as the truth remains stubbornly out of reach.

What endures is not just a mystery—but a name that refuses to be reduced to one.

CHAPTER 12 LAW ENFORCEMENT THEN AND NOW

When disappeared in 2000, law enforcement faced a case shaped as much by what *wasn't* available as by what was.

At the time, investigative tools were limited by the era. There were no widespread surveillance cameras. No GPS data from personal devices. No social media footprints to analyze. Cell phone records, when they existed, were sparse and difficult to access. For a child of nine, there was virtually no digital trail at all.

What investigators had instead were witness statements, physical searches, and traditional detective work—and even those were compromised by the storm that night. Rain erased tracks. Wind scattered scent. Time slipped through their hands.

From the beginning, local law enforcement worked alongside state and federal agencies, including the FBI. The case was treated seriously, not as a runaway but as a missing child under suspicious circumstances. Resources were mobilized quickly. Leads were pursued. But progress stalled almost as soon as it began.

As years passed, the case transitioned from active emergency to long-term investigation.

Cold cases are not abandoned—but they do change.

Files grow thicker. Tips slow. Personnel rotate. Knowledge must be preserved through documentation rather than memory. In Asha's case, investigators had to ensure that no detail—no matter how small—was lost to time.

The discovery of the backpack in 2001 renewed momentum, but it also highlighted the limitations of the forensic tools available at the time. DNA testing was far less advanced. Trace evidence that might yield answers today could not be fully analyzed then.

That gap has never been forgotten.

Over the years, law enforcement has revisited physical evidence as technology improved. Items were reexamined. New techniques applied. Old conclusions reassessed. Investigators publicly acknowledged that advances in forensic science could still change the trajectory of the case.

But science alone cannot solve what evidence does not reveal.

The greatest challenge has always been the same: there is no known point of violence. No confirmed moment where Asha was taken. No verified witness who saw her enter a vehicle or encounter another person.

Without that anchor, the investigation floats.

Law enforcement continues to emphasize that the case remains open. Periodic public appeals are made. Age-progressed images are released. Investigators encourage anyone with information—no matter how insignificant it may seem—to come forward.

Because in cases like this, truth often arrives late.

Sometimes it comes from a conscience burdened by time.

Sometimes from a memory unlocked by a news story. Sometimes from someone finally realizing that what they once saw or heard mattered more than they understood.

For investigators, Asha Degree's case represents both determination and humility. Determination to keep searching. Humility in acknowledging that not all mysteries yield quickly—or cleanly—to human effort.

The tools have changed.

The commitment has not.

And somewhere, buried in memory or hidden in silence, law enforcement believes the missing piece still exists—waiting to be spoken.

CHAPTER 13 WHAT WE KNOW FOR CERTAIN

After decades of investigation, speculation, and unanswered questions, the case of rests on a small but solid foundation of facts.

Everything else—no matter how compelling—must be measured against them.

Asha Left Her Home on Her Own Feet

There is no evidence of forced entry. No sign of a struggle inside the Degree home. Doors were locked. Windows intact. Family members were asleep. Asha was not taken from her bed.

She left.

How willingly remains unknown, but the act itself is certain.

She Was Seen Walking Along Highway 18

Multiple motorists independently reported seeing a child matching Asha's description walking south along Highway 18 in the early hours of February 14, 2000. Their accounts were consistent in timing and location.

One driver's attempt to approach her ended with Asha running into the woods.

This was not a rumor.

It was corroborated.

She Reached the Area Near the Shed

Items belonging to Asha were found in a storage shed near where she was last seen. This confirms that she survived the walk and sought shelter—or at least stopped—in that area.

Whatever happened to her did not occur immediately after she left the road.

Her Backpack Was Moved and Hidden

Eighteen months later, Asha's backpack was found buried in another county, wrapped in plastic. The condition and placement strongly suggest intentional concealment by another person.

This is one of the clearest indicators that Asha did not simply wander off and perish unnoticed.

Her Family Was Cleared

Law enforcement thoroughly investigated the Degree family and found no evidence of involvement. They cooperated fully and remain victims, not suspects.

This conclusion has not changed.

There Is No Confirmed Witness Beyond the Highway

After Asha ran into the woods, no verified sighting places her with another person. No one saw her enter a vehicle. No one heard a struggle. No one came forward with direct knowledge of her fate.

That silence defines the case.

The Case Remains Open

Despite years without resolution, Asha Degree's disappearance has never been closed or classified as resolved. Investigators continue to consider it active.

That status matters.

It means law enforcement believes answers are still possible.

What the Facts Tell Us—and What They Don't

The known facts draw a narrow corridor through a wide field of uncertainty. They tell us where Asha was. They tell us when she was last seen. They tell us that someone likely intervened after she left the shed area.

They do not tell us *why* she left, *who* she encountered, or *what* ultimately happened to her.

Certainty in this case is not abundant.

But it exists.

LINDA DAVIDSON

And it is the only ground on which the truth can eventually stand.

CHAPTER 14
THE QUESTIONS THAT HAUNT

Every unresolved case leaves questions behind.

But some cases seem built from them.

In the disappearance of , the questions do not sit quietly at the edges of the story. They occupy its center, pressing in from all sides, demanding attention while refusing to yield answers.

The first question is also the most unsettling.

Why Did She Leave?

Asha did not leave in anger. There was no argument, no punishment, no moment of visible distress. She did not storm out or act impulsively. She waited until her house was asleep. She packed a bag. She chose a time when discovery would be delayed.

What could have motivated a nine-year-old to do that?

Was she responding to something immediate—fear, urgency,

instruction—or something planned, however imperfectly? Was she trying to reach a specific place, or was the act of leaving itself the goal?

No explanation fully accounts for her age, her personality, and the conditions she faced that night.

Where Was She Going?

Children who leave home usually go somewhere familiar: a friend's house, a relative's home, a place they associate with safety.

Asha did not.

Highway 18 was not a route to comfort. It did not lead to school, church, or a known destination she frequented. There was no logical endpoint for a child on foot in the middle of the night.

If she believed she was going somewhere specific, that destination has never been identified.

And if she wasn't—if she was simply following instructions or instinct—then the danger she walked into becomes even more profound.

Why Did She Run From Help?

The moment she fled from the approaching car remains one of the most psychologically troubling aspects of the case.

Children in danger usually seek adults. They flag them down. They cry. They cling.

Asha ran.

Was she afraid of strangers? Afraid of getting in trouble? Afraid of something—or someone—she believed was worse than the driver?

That choice suggests a mindset shaped by fear, belief, or conditioning strong enough to override survival instincts.

What Happened After the Shed?

The shed marks the last place where Asha's presence can be confirmed.

After that, there is nothing.

No path. No timeline. No witness.

Did she leave on her own? Was she approached? Did she meet someone she expected—or someone she didn't? Was the encounter brief or prolonged?

The buried backpack suggests a later intervention, but it does not reveal when or where that intervention occurred.

Who Knows More Than They've Said?

In nearly every long-unsolved case, there is an unspoken assumption: someone, somewhere, knows something.

A comment dismissed. A memory suppressed. A detail once thought irrelevant.

The challenge is not just finding that person—but reaching the moment when silence becomes heavier than truth.

The Weight of Unanswered Questions

These questions persist not because investigators failed to ask them, but because the answers remain hidden—locked in time, memory, or intention.

They haunt the family who wakes up each day without closure.

They haunt investigators who revisit the file, hoping something finally aligns.

They haunt a public that cannot reconcile how a child could vanish so completely.

Asha Degree's story does not end with a solution.

It ends with an open door—one that still waits for someone to step forward, to speak, to remember.

Until then, the questions remain.

And so does the hope that one day, they won't.

EPILOGUE

— *A Name That Never Faded*

There are cases that end with a courtroom.

There are cases that end with a confession.

And then there are cases like , where the ending never arrives —only the passage of time, carrying the same questions forward year after year.

In Shelby, North Carolina, time kept moving in all the ways it always does. Seasons changed. Children grew up. Schools welcomed new classes who had never known the name Asha Degree until a teacher mentioned it, until a poster appeared in a hallway, until an anniversary story aired on the news. Life continued—not because the community stopped caring, but because life has a relentless way of continuing even when a wound remains open.

For Asha's family, the years did not erase her.

They learned to exist in the presence of absence. They learned how to answer questions no parent should ever have to answer: *How many years has it been? What do you think happened? Do you still hope?* They learned how to live in the tension between faith and uncertainty, between endurance and exhaustion.

They also learned that grief can be public.

In missing child cases, families often become symbols—of hope, of tragedy, of mystery. Their pain becomes part of the narrative people consume. Some strangers offer sincere compassion. Others offer suspicion dressed as curiosity. And even when the world moves on, the family remains, carrying a story that never gives them the mercy of closure.

Yet the Degree family continued to speak Asha's name.

Because silence, in a case like this, can feel like surrender.

Law enforcement never closed the file. The case remained active, revisited as leads emerged and technology evolved. Each new method, each new tip line call, each fresh wave of attention brought the possibility—however small—that the next piece of information might finally be the one that mattered.

The public's relationship with the case shifted over time. In the early days, it was local urgency. Then regional attention. Then long-term fascination. Asha's disappearance became one of those haunting American mysteries that refuses to settle into the past.

Part of that is because the case is so stark.

A child left a home in the night.

She was seen walking in the rain.

She ran into the woods.

And then she was gone.

It is a story that does not behave the way stories are supposed to.

And in that refusal—its lack of resolution, its lack of certainty—Asha Degree becomes more than a headline. She becomes a reminder. Of how fragile safety can be. Of how quickly normal life can tilt into chaos. Of how many disappearances begin without warning and end without answers.

But Asha was not a mystery first.

She was a child.

A girl who went to school, who played basketball, who lived in a home where the day-to-day felt steady. A girl who mattered long before the world learned her name. A girl who is still loved, still searched for, still held in memory by people who refuse to let the story become only a question mark.

The truth is, this case is not finished.

It is unfinished.

And that distinction matters.

Because unfinished means there is still room for an answer—somewhere. In someone's memory. In a forgotten detail. In a withheld confession. In a piece of evidence waiting to speak louder than it once could. In a quiet moment when someone decides that the cost of silence has finally become too high.

Until that day comes, Asha Degree remains what she has always been in this story: a child at the center of a night that never truly ended.

And her name—spoken in vigils, printed on flyers, carried in prayers, repeated year after year—does what mystery cannot.

It keeps her human.

It keeps her present.

It refuses to let her disappear completely.

A PERSONAL REQUEST

Thank you for reading **Gone Before Morning: The Unanswered Case of Asha Degree**.

If this book stayed with you, I would be deeply grateful if you left a review. Even a simple star rating—without writing anything else—matters more than most readers realize. It helps bookstores and platforms understand that this story is important, and it helps thoughtful, victim-centered true crime reach the right audience.

If you'd like to leave a review, you can visit the Amazon page here:

Gone Before Morning: The Unanswered Case of Asha Degree

Or simply scan the QR code below to go directly to the review page:

Your support helps keep attention where it belongs—on Asha, on the family who has waited for answers, and on the truth that still deserves daylight.

With gratitude,

Linda Davidson

THE GONE BEFORE SERIES

True Crime Disappearances at the Edge of Ordinary Time

Gone Before the Shift Ended: The Unanswered Disappearance of Patti Adkins

A factory worker vanishes after her night shift, leaving behind secrets, suspicion, and a case still clouded in silence.

Gone Before Morning: The Unanswered Case of Asha Degree

A nine-year-old girl walks into the dark before dawn — and is never seen again.

Gone Before Sunrise: The Disappearance of Holly Bobo

A young nursing student is led into the woods at daybreak, sparking one of Tennessee's most haunting investigations.

APPENDIX A — CASE TIMELINE AT A GLANCE

Sunday, February 13, 2000 (Evening)

- Asha spends the day with her family (church/community routines, normal home life).
- Weather worsens overnight; rain and wind move in.
- A power outage affects the area that night.

Late Night / Early Morning, February 14, 2000

- Asha goes to bed in the shared room with her brother.
- **Sometime after the household is asleep (approx. 2:30–3:30 a.m.)** Asha leaves the home with a backpack.
- **Before dawn (approx. 3:30–4:30 a.m.)** motorists report seeing a child matching Asha's description walking along **Highway 18**.
- One driver turns around; the child **runs off the road into the woods**.

February 14, 2000 (Morning)

- Asha is discovered missing.
- Police are notified; initial searches begin.
- Search scope expands rapidly based on the highway sightings.

Days After the Disappearance

- Large volunteer searches, K-9 units, and aerial support focus around the Highway 18 corridor.
- Items consistent with Asha's belongings are later

reported in/near a roadside shed area connected to the last sighting zone.

August 2001 (Approx. 18 Months Later)

- Asha's backpack is discovered **buried** in another county, wrapped in plastic bags.
- The case surges back into public attention; evidence is re-evaluated.

Years and Ongoing

- The case remains open.
- Tips continue intermittently.
- Evidence is revisited as investigative methods improve.

APPENDIX B — KEY LOCATIONS AND WHY THEY MATTER

1) The Degree Home (Shelby area)
- The last confirmed safe location.
- Critical because there was **no forced entry** and no immediate sign of struggle—suggesting Asha left the house without obvious violence inside the home.

2) Neighborhood Route to Highway 18
- The "silent corridor" between home and highway.
- If anyone encountered Asha close to home, this is where it likely happened—yet it produced little confirmable evidence.

3) Highway 18 Sightings Corridor
- The last confirmed public sightings.
- Important because multiple motorists saw a child walking alone in the early morning rain—supporting that Asha was moving on foot.

4) Woods / Run-Off Point
- Where Asha ran from a vehicle and disappeared into darkness.
- This point is psychologically and investigatively critical: it suggests fear, urgency, or a determination to avoid contact.

5) The Shed Area

- The first place where physical items associated with the disappearance are discussed as having been found.
- Significant because it implies Asha may have **stopped**—seeking shelter, hiding, or pausing before something changed.

6) Backpack Recovery Site (Burke County area)

- Far from the last sightings.
- The backpack being wrapped and buried strongly suggests **intentional concealment**, shifting the case from "lost child" possibilities toward human involvement.

APPENDIX C — MYTHS VS. FACTS

Myth: "She must have been a typical runaway."

Reality: Asha was nine years old and described as cautious, family-oriented, and not known for rebellious behavior. The circumstances don't neatly match a common runaway pattern.

Myth: "There were no witnesses at all."

Reality: Multiple motorists reported seeing a child walking along Highway 18 before dawn, and one reported the child ran into the woods.

Myth: "The family was never investigated."

Reality: The family was investigated and repeatedly questioned early on (as is standard in missing child cases) and was **not treated as responsible** based on the available information.

Myth: "The backpack proves exactly what happened."

Reality: The backpack is powerful evidence—but it's not a full explanation. It suggests movement and concealment, but it does not reveal who, when, or why.

Myth: "Internet rumors are 'hidden facts' authorities won't share."

Reality: Most rumors arise from repetition, misquotes, or speculation. In an open case, many details are withheld not for drama, but to protect investigative integrity and avoid contaminating tips.

APPENDIX D — HOW COLD CASES GET REOPENED AND SOLVED

Cold cases don't "wake up" all at once. They usually move when **one** of these shifts happens:

1) A New Witness Speaks

- Someone's guilt changes.
- Someone's fear fades.
- Someone realizes an old memory wasn't "nothing."

2) New Forensic Testing

- Evidence that was once untestable becomes testable.
- Old samples are re-run using improved methods.
- Small trace evidence becomes meaningful as science advances.

3) A Pattern Emerges

- Investigators notice similarities with another case.
- A known offender's history or geography suddenly aligns.
- A vehicle or location becomes relevant again due to new context.

4) A Tip Becomes Verifiable

- Tips are common; **verifiable** tips are rare.
- A single detail that can be checked—an address, a name, a photo, a location—can change everything.

5) Evidence Reinterpretation

- Fresh eyes review old files.
- A timeline is corrected.
- A "minor" item becomes a major lead when seen differently.

6) Public Attention Sparks the Right Memory

- Media can be messy, but it can also jog someone's conscience or memory.
- One person seeing a recap can trigger: "I remember that night… and that car… and that person…"

APPENDIX E — FACTS-ONLY NARRATIVE TIMELINE (REPORT STYLE)

Case: Asha Jaquilla Degree

Location: Shelby, Cleveland County, North Carolina (U.S.)

Date of Disappearance: February 14, 2000

Status: Open / Unresolved

Sunday, February 13, 2000 (Evening)

Asha Degree, age 9, is at home with her family. The evening is described as routine for the household. Weather conditions worsen overnight, with rain and wind reported in the area. A power outage is reported in the region that night.

Late Night to Early Morning (February 13–14, 2000)

Asha goes to bed in a bedroom she shares with her brother. During the overnight hours, after other members of the household are asleep, Asha leaves the residence. She departs with a backpack. No confirmed forced entry into the home is reported in connection with the disappearance.

Pre-Dawn Hours, Monday, February 14, 2000

Motorists report seeing a child believed to match Asha's description walking along a stretch of Highway 18 before dawn. At least one motorist reports turning a vehicle around; the child reportedly leaves the roadway and runs into nearby woods. No confirmed contact is reported between Asha and any driver.

Morning of February 14, 2000
Asha is discovered missing from her home. Law enforcement is

APPENDIX F — GLOSSARY OF RECURRING TERMS

This glossary explains key investigative and legal terms that appear throughout this book. The goal is clarity—not technical complexity.

Amber Alert

A public emergency notification system used in cases involving abducted children who are believed to be in immediate danger.

Burden of Proof

The obligation to prove an allegation in court. In criminal cases, the prosecution must prove guilt beyond a reasonable doubt.

Case File

The official collection of reports, witness statements, evidence logs, lab results, and internal notes related to an investigation.

Cold Case

A criminal investigation that remains unsolved after active leads have been exhausted. Cold cases are periodically reviewed when new evidence, technology, or tips emerge.

Concealment

An intentional act of hiding evidence, a body, or items connected to a crime.

Corroboration

Independent confirmation of a fact. For example, when one witness statement is supported by physical evidence or another verified account.

Evidence (Physical Evidence)

Any tangible object or material collected during an investigation that may help establish facts—such as clothing, DNA, fingerprints, fibers, or personal belongings.

Forensic Testing

Scientific examination of evidence (e.g., DNA analysis, fingerprint comparison, trace analysis) to assist in identifying individuals or reconstructing events.

Jurisdiction

The geographic area or authority under which a specific law enforcement agency operates.

K-9 Unit

A law enforcement team that includes specially trained dogs used for tracking, scent detection, and search operations.

Last Known Location (LKL)

The most recent confirmed place where a missing person was seen or verified to be safe.

Lead

Information that may help advance an investigation. Leads require verification before being considered reliable.

Missing Persons Case

An investigation initiated when a person's whereabouts are unknown and their safety cannot be confirmed.

Open Case

An investigation that remains active and unresolved.

Person of Interest

An individual whom law enforcement believes may have relevant information about a case but who has not been formally charged with a crime.

Probable Cause

A reasonable basis for believing that a crime may have been committed, required for certain legal actions such as issuing search or arrest warrants.

Search Perimeter

A defined geographic area established during a search operation where investigators focus resources.

Timeline

A structured sequence of verified events arranged chronologically to help clarify when and how events unfolded.

Tip Line

A phone number, email address, or online portal designated for the public to submit information related to a case.

Unidentified Remains

Human remains that have not yet been conclusively identified.

Verification

The process of confirming information through reliable sources, documentation, or evidence.

This glossary is intended to make investigative language more accessible. Understanding terminology helps readers evaluate information carefully and distinguish between verified facts, informed analysis, and speculation.

ACKNOWLEDGMENTS

This book was written with deep respect for the life of Asha Degree and for every family living with unanswered questions. A child's absence is not a mystery to be consumed—it is a life interrupted, a family changed forever, and a question that doesn't stop echoing when the headlines move on. While a single book cannot carry the full weight of that loss, it can hold space for memory, protect the record from distortion, and keep attention where it belongs: on the person who did not come home.

First and foremost, I acknowledge Asha. Not as a case, not as a headline, but as a nine-year-old girl whose life mattered—whose presence mattered—whose name deserves to be spoken with care.

To Asha's family, and to all families who live with the long, relentless ache of not knowing: I recognize the courage it takes to endure a silence that never resolves. Grief is hard enough when there is an ending; unanswered grief is its own kind of endurance. This book does not claim to give what has never been given. It exists in part to honor the truth that a family can keep loving, hoping, and searching through years that the rest of the world counts and forgets.

I want to acknowledge the investigators, search teams, volunteers, and community members who have worked—publicly and privately—to keep this case active. In missing-person cases, the work is often quiet and thankless: walking wooded edges, reviewing files, following tips that lead nowhere, returning again and again to the same unanswered ground. The persistence itself matters. Even when answers do not arrive, effort is not meaningless. It is a refusal to accept disappearance as normal.

I also acknowledge the journalists, archivists, librarians, and local record-keepers who have preserved timelines, documents, and coverage over decades. In a case shaped by time, memory can blur and rumors can harden into "truth" through repetition. The people who preserve the original record—however incomplete it may be—help protect both the investigation and the dignity of the person at its center.

This book is also written in recognition of the many missing children whose names never reach national attention—children whose disappearances are treated as smaller because their families have fewer resources, less visibility, or less institutional urgency on their side. Every child is a whole world to someone. Every absence deserves seriousness. Every family deserves to be heard.

Finally, I acknowledge the readers who approach true crime with empathy and care—readers who resist voyeurism, who value accuracy over rumor, and who understand that behind every case file is a human being whose life mattered. If you read with patience, humility, and respect, you become part of what keeps a story from turning into spectacle. You help make space for memory. And sometimes, awareness—responsible awareness—keeps a case from fading.

Thank you for reading with your humanity intact.

DISCLAIMER

Gone Before Morning: The Unanswered Case of Asha Degree is a work of nonfiction based on publicly available records, media reporting, interviews, and documented investigative updates available at the time of writing. Every reasonable effort has been made to verify dates, timelines, and factual details. Any remaining errors are unintentional and are the responsibility of the author.

This book addresses the disappearance of a minor and discusses themes that may be distressing, including missing persons, child vulnerability, and investigative uncertainty. Reader discretion is advised. Graphic detail has been intentionally limited out of respect for the child at the center of this case and for her family.

This case remains open. Where theories, interpretations, or investigative possibilities are discussed, they are presented as such—not as established fact. Allegations referenced from historical reporting are identified as allegations and should not be interpreted as findings of guilt. No individual is declared responsible unless formally charged and adjudicated in a court of law.

In limited instances, minor contextual details that are not central to the factual record may be condensed or clarified for narrative flow. Such adjustments do not alter the documented substance of the case.

This book does not provide legal, investigative, or professional advice. Discussions of law enforcement procedure, forensic methods, and cold case practices are included for informational purposes only.

The intent of this work is remembrance, clarity, and responsible examination—not speculation or sensationalism. The focus remains on preserving verified information, honoring Asha Degree, and encouraging continued awareness in an unresolved case.

Any included URLs or external references were active at the time of publication but may change over time.

This book is an independent work and is not affiliated with or endorsed by any law enforcement agency or institution mentioned herein.

AUTHOR'S NOTE

This book is a narrative true-crime account based on publicly available information, reported timelines, and known case developments. In an unresolved investigation, certain details may be withheld by authorities, disputed in sources, or difficult to verify conclusively.

Where uncertainty exists, this book aims to treat it honestly —distinguishing confirmed facts from theory and rumor. Some scenes have been presented in a narrative style to help readers understand sequence and emotional stakes; however, the intent throughout is to remain faithful to the known record and to avoid sensationalism.

If you have credible information related to this case, consider contacting the appropriate law enforcement agency.

READER DISCRETION STATEMENT

This book involves the disappearance of a child and may contain material that is emotionally difficult. Reader discretion is advised.

NOTES ON TERMINOLOGY AND APPROACH

- **"Confirmed"** refers to details corroborated by official statements or widely consistent reporting across reputable sources.
- **"Reported"** refers to details described in media accounts and community reporting but not publicly verified in full.
- **"Theory"** refers to proposed explanations that remain unproven.

This approach is intended to honor the seriousness of an open case and protect readers from misinformation disguised as certainty.

ABOUT THE AUTHOR

Linda Davidson is a true crime author who writes for readers who want more than shock value — they want truth with a heartbeat.

She focuses on the kinds of stories that stay with you long after the news cameras leave: unsolved murders, missing persons, rural disappearances, and investigations that never received clear answers. Instead of chasing sensational headlines, Linda writes with one question in mind: *How can I honor the victim and still tell the full truth of what happened?*

In each book, she blends careful research, clear timelines, and compassionate storytelling. Readers are guided through evidence, leads, theories, and dead ends in a way that is easy to follow and emotionally grounded. Her work keeps the victim at the center of the narrative while also examining the failures, gaps, and human decisions that shaped each case.

Linda's books are written for true crime readers who care about people, not just plot twists. She writes for those who feel frustrated by shallow coverage and are hungry for deeper, more thoughtful explorations of the cases that haunt them.

Her promise is simple:

She will research carefully.

She will explain clearly.

She will tell the truth with respect.

She will never forget that the people she writes about were real.

Linda Davidson is a true crime author dedicated to telling

the stories others forget. She writes about unsolved murders, mysterious disappearances, and cold cases with a focus on the victims, their families, and the communities left behind. Combining deep research with compassionate storytelling, she helps readers make sense of complex investigations without losing sight of the human beings at the center of every case.

ALSO BY LINDA DAVIDSON

1. The Zodiac Killer Never Caught: The Crimes, the Ciphers, and the Search for Justice
2. The Black Dahlia: Reclaiming Elizabeth Short
3. Down the Hill: The Girls Who Captured a Killer — and the Secrets Still Buried in Delphi
4. Justice Denied: JonBenét Ramsey Mystery
5. Red Light Vanish: The Disappearance of Bryce Laspisa and the Night That Still Haunts California
6. Don't Let Me Die Here: The Lars Mittank Case — A True Story of Disappearance, Fear, and a Mother's Unbreakable Hope
7. The Vanished Heiress: Agatha Christie's Eleven Days of Silence
8. Without a Trace: The Cold silence of Maura Murray
9. Charming the Darkness: The Rodney Alcala Case
10. Whispers Along the Parkway: The Unsolved Murders That Haunt America's Cradle of History
11. *Vanished on the Open Road: The Gabby Petito Story*
12. Bloodline Broken: The Fall of the Murdaugh Dynasty
13. Buried in the Sand: Thirteen Victims. One Quiet Monster. A Decade of Silence
14. *Stolen Faces: The Man Who Became the Missing*
15. *The Glamour Grift: How Anna Delvey Fooled the Rich and Faked Her Empire*
16. *The Last Mile He Walked: A True Story of Loss, Confusion and The Disappearance of Brandon Swanson*

17. *Tracks to Nowhere: The Mysterious Death of Tiffany Valiante*
18. *Buried in Belief : The Shocking Crimes of Lori Vallow and Chad Daybell*
19. *Tracks to Nowhere: The Mysterious Death of Tiffany Valiante*
20. *Silent Blocks: The Disappearance of Jason Jolkowski and the Walk He Never Finished*

A FINAL WORD TO THE READER

If you've reached the end of this book, you've carried Asha's name for a while. That matters.

Unresolved cases rely on memory—on people who keep the story alive long enough for the truth to surface. Sometimes it is one sentence, one recollection, one small detail finally spoken aloud that breaks a case open.

Until then, the most powerful thing we can do is remember: Asha was not a mystery first. She was a child—loved, known, and missing.

FOLLOW THE AUTHOR

To explore all of Linda Davidson's books and new releases, visit her Amazon Author Page on Kindle: Linda Davidson.

END NOTE

— *Light in the Dark*

Stories like this one walk us through some of the darkest places a human heart can go. It is easy to believe that evil has the last word—that violence, corruption, or indifference are stronger than anything else.

The Bible says something different. It tells us that God sees every unseen hurt, hears every unheard prayer, and judges every hidden deed. It also says that no life is beyond His reach, and no story is too broken to be redeemed. Justice matters to God. So does mercy. So does you.

If what you've read has stirred fear, anger, or regret in your own heart, know this: the door back to Him is never closed. Repentance is simply turning around and letting Him meet you where you are.

"Do not be overcome by evil, but overcome evil with good."

— Romans 12:21

"The light shines in the darkness, and the darkness has not overcome it."

— John 1:5

May these pages not only expose what went wrong, but also awaken a hunger for what is right—for justice, for truth, and for the kind of grace that can still save a soul.

APPEAL FOR INFORMATION

The disappearance of remains an open and active investigation.

If you have *any* information—no matter how small or uncertain it may seem—related to Asha's disappearance, law enforcement urges you to come forward. Details that once felt insignificant can become critical when viewed in a new context or combined with other information.

You may have:

- Seen a child walking along Highway 18 in the early morning hours of February 14, 2000
- Noticed an unfamiliar vehicle parked along the road or in a rural area that night or in the days that followed
- Heard a comment, rumor, or confession that troubled you but felt unsure how to report
- Remembered a detail years later that now feels different in light of what is known
- Had involvement or knowledge you were afraid to share at the time

Time does not erase truth.

If fear, uncertainty, loyalty, or doubt once kept you silent, know that investigators continue to seek answers—not judgment. Information can be provided confidentially.

HOW TO REPORT INFORMATION

If you have information related to this case, please contact:

- **Cleveland County Sheriff's Office**
- **North Carolina State Bureau of Investigation (SBI)**
- **FBI Tip Line** (for information crossing state lines)

If you are unsure whether what you know matters, report it anyway.

Let investigators decide.

A FINAL REMINDER

This case did not end in 2000.

Someone, somewhere, knows something that has not yet been spoken.

Your voice—your memory—may be the missing piece.

REFERENCES

Charlotte Observer. (2024, September 13). Large-scale search in Shelby: FBI, SBI and local law enforcement linked to Asha Degree case. *The Charlotte Observer.*

Coin, J. (2025, February 12). "Wounds never closed": NC town reflects on 25 years of unsolved Asha Degree disappearance. *The Charlotte Observer.*

Coin, J. (2025, February 20). New court records provide details in Asha Degree case. *The Charlotte Observer.*

Federal Bureau of Investigation. (2020, February 14). Looking for Asha. *FBI.*

Federal Bureau of Investigation. (n.d.). Asha Degree age-progression by the National Center for Missing & Exploited Children (video). *FBI.* (Retrieved February 10, 2026)

National Center for Missing & Exploited Children. (n.d.). Have you seen this child? Asha Jaquilla Degree. *missingkids.org.* (Retrieved February 10, 2026)

National Center for Missing & Exploited Children. (2020, February 14). The search continues for Asha Degree. *missingkids.org.*

North Carolina State Bureau of Investigation. (n.d.). Asha Jaquilla Degree. *NCSBI.gov.* (Retrieved February 10, 2026)

WSOC-TV. (2024, September 13). Sheriff confirms new search warrants, items seized in Asha Degree case. *WSOC-TV.*

WBTV. (2025, February 18). New Asha Degree warrants: Text messages revealed, possible admission of fault, more. *WBTV.*

WBTV. (2025, February 21). Asha Degree case: No comment from attorney of family involved as investigation unfolds. *WBTV*.

WBTV. (2025, April 4). Large law enforcement presence in Cherryville tied to Asha Degree investigation: What we know. *WBTV*.

WBTV. (2025, September 26). Reward increased to $100K for information in Asha Degree's disappearance. *WBTV*.

WXII 12 News. (2025, April 4). Asha Degree: Investigators search property once owned by prominent figure in case. *WXII 12 News*.

FURTHER READING AND VIEWING

Federal Bureau of Investigation. (2020, February 14). Looking for Asha. *FBI*.

National Center for Missing & Exploited Children. (n.d.). Have you seen this child? Asha Jaquilla Degree (NCMEC poster). *missingkids.org*. (Retrieved February 10, 2026)

National Center for Missing & Exploited Children. (2020, February 14). The search continues for Asha Degree. *missingkids.org*.

North Carolina State Bureau of Investigation. (n.d.). Asha Jaquilla Degree. *NCSBI.gov*. (Retrieved February 10, 2026)

Spectrum Local News. (2025, April 4). FBI, SBI join search at new locations in Asha Degree case. *Spectrum News 1*.

Wikipedia contributors. (n.d.). Disappearance of Asha Degree. *Wikipedia*. (Retrieved February 10, 2026)

(Useful as a navigation hub for names/dates, but always verify details against primary reporting.)

FURTHER VIEWING AND LISTENING

(documentaries, video, podcasts)

Federal Bureau of Investigation. (2022, February 14). Inside the FBI: Searching for Asha Degree (audio episode). *FBI*.

Federal Bureau of Investigation. (n.d.). Asha Degree age-progression by the National Center for Missing & Exploited Children (video). *FBI*. (Retrieved February 10, 2026)

Find Our Missing. (2013, February 18). Asha Degree and Kelly Allen (Season 1, Episode 2). *IMDb*. (Retrieved February 10, 2026)

The Valentine's Vanishing. (n.d.). The unresolved disappearance of Asha Degree. *Apple TV*. (Retrieved February 10, 2026)

Crime Junkie. (n.d.). MISSING: Asha Degree. *audiochuck*. (Retrieved February 10, 2026)

True Crime Garage. (2025, March 4). Asha Degree (Part 1) (Episode 826). *Apple Podcasts*.

Spotify. (2025, May 28). VANISHED: Asha Degree. *Spotify*. (Retrieved February 10, 2026)

Printed in Dunstable, United Kingdom